The Climate
of Learning

The John Dewey Society Lectureship Series

The John Dewey Society Lecture is delivered annually under the sponsorship of the John Dewey Society at the annual meeting of the National Society of College Teachers of Education. Arrangements for the presentation and publication of the Lecture are under the direction of the John Dewey Society Commission on Publications.

ARCHIBALD W. ANDERSON, University of Illinois,
Chairman and Editor

R. FREEMAN BUTTS, Teachers College, Columbia University

CARTER HARRISON, Boston University

HAROLD SHANE, Northwestern University

WILLIAM O. STANLEY, University of Illinois

LINDLEY J. STILES, University of Wisconsin

The John Dewey Society Lectureship—Number One

The Climate of Learning

A Constructive Attack on Complacency in Higher Education

by

ORDWAY TEAD

Foreword by
ARCHIBALD W. ANDERSON
*Chairman, The John Dewey Society
Commission on Publications*

HARPER & BROTHERS
NEW YORK

378.01
T 25

49637

THE CLIMATE OF LEARNING

Copyright © 1958 by Harper & Brothers

Printed in the United States of America

All rights in this book are reserved.
No part of the book may be used or reproduced
in any manner whatsoever without written per-
mission except in the case of brief quotations
embodied in critical articles and reviews. For
information address Harper & Brothers
49 East 33rd Street, New York 16, N. Y.

B-I

Library of Congress catalog card number: 58-11046

Foreword

BY ARCHIBALD W. ANDERSON

*Chairman, The John Dewey Society Commission
on Publications*

The establishment of an annual lectureship is a new but logical extension of the activities of the John Dewey Society for the Study of Education and Culture. As the full name of the organization implies, and as one of its official publications explicitly states, "The John Dewey Society was established to foster the study of democratic education in its relationship with the culture, and to promote thorough and systematic inquiry and investigation in the social foundations of education."

Although the Society has never ceased its efforts to achieve the purpose for which it was created in 1935, there has been growth and development in the Society's perception of the nature of that purpose and in the Society's judgment concerning the means most appropriate for achieving it. This evolution is a direct outcome of the Society's dedication to the exploration of the frontier problems of education and the culture. As education and the culture have changed, the frontier problems have changed. In order to remain faithful to its original purpose, the Society has had to expand and modify its approach to those problems.

Increasingly, in recent years, the John Dewey Society has focused on the study of educational theory, and on investigation and inquiry into the theoretical foundations of education. It is here that the Society has found frontier problems that urgently need exploration.

Although public education had seemed to be jeopardized by the postwar waves of attack launched against it, the aftermath of this period of attack was actually a situation in which basic issues of educational theory could be discussed with greater hope of reaching a wider audience than had earlier been the case. Certainly, the middle of the twentieth century has been characterized by the greatest public discussion of education since the great debates of the nineteenth century over the founding of public school systems. And the issues around which the current debate has tended to center are not details of educational practice but rather those fundamental issues of educational policy which can be resolved only as the basic issues in educational theory are explored in such a way as to give a sound basis for making the necessary decisions about educational policy.

In short, this is a period of great educational problems. It could be a period of danger if the resources for dealing with the problems are not found. It can be a period of great advance if these resources are found and used. It is the belief of the John Dewey Society that such an advance is realistically possible.

William Heard Kilpatrick has epitomized the potentialities of such a period in an article on "John Dewey and His Educational Theory," written for the October, 1952, number of *Progressive Education*. In speaking of the situation which existed at the time when Dewey began his career, Professor Kilpatrick said, "Great creative thinking, it seems fair to assert, arises only in the face of great problems, and, even then, best if not only as there appear available at the same time new and promising thought resources."

In the hope of fostering the creative thinking about education which the present situation demands, the John Dewey Society has decided to establish two new publication series.

One of these is the *John Dewey Society Studies in Educational Theory*. This is to consist of books, published annually, in which one or two authors make a vigorous and searching study of some significant problem in, or contributing to, the theoretical foundations of education.

The second of the new series is the *John Dewey Society Lectureship Series*. This is to consist of the printed version of an annual lecture to be delivered by some outstanding individual, either in or outside the field of education, whose ideas could be regarded as one of the thought resources to be explored by those seeking to advance the theory of education.

Since the John Dewey Society has followed the policy of sponsoring meetings only in cooperation with some other educational organization, it set out to find the proper forum for the presentation of what was intended to be a significant statement on education. In the present instance, it was possible to make a cooperative arrangement with the National Society of College Teachers of Education under which this organization would make available each year one of the general sessions of its annual convention for the presentation of the John Dewey Society Lecture. The first lecture under this joint arrangement was delivered in Chicago on February 21, 1958. An expanded version of this lecture is presented in the present volume.

The John Dewey Society feels that the lecturer it was able to secure, Dr. Ordway Tead, and the subject he chose to discuss, *The Climate of Learning: A Constructive Attack on Complacency in Higher Education,* have both fully justified the expectations it entertained when it established the Lectureship Series. Dr. Tead is one of those rare individuals who, with apparent ease, can carry on several professions and occupations at the same time. This gives an unusual comprehensiveness to his approach to education. He can approach an educational problem as a businessman. He can approach it as an editor and author. And he can approach it as an educator in the dual capacity of teacher and administrator.

A graduate of Amherst College, Dr. Tead holds the LL.D. degree from St. Lawrence University, Keuka College, the American International College, and Northwestern University; the L.H.D. degree from Amherst College, Brooklyn College, and Columbia University; and the Litt. D. degree from Bard College.

Dr. Tead's editorial career has included work as Director of Business Publications for McGraw-Hill Book Company from 1920 to 1925 and Editor of Social and Economic Books for Harper and Brothers since 1925. He is also a Vice President and Director of the latter firm. He is the author of nearly a dozen books and numerous magazine articles. The titles of his books cover personnel administration, business management, industrial and labor relations, school administration, and higher education.

As a teacher, Dr. Tead was a member of the Department of Industry at the New York School of Social Work from 1920 to 1929, and a lecturer on Personnel Administration at Columbia University from 1920 to 1950. From 1950 to 1956 he has been Adjunct Professor of Industrial Relations at Columbia. His connection with the administration of higher education has been as Chairman of the Board of Higher Education of New York City for fifteen years and as Chairman of the Board of Trustees of Briarcliff College for sixteen years. Dr. Tead has served as a member of the Executive Board of the Institute of International Education, as a member and consultant to the President's Commission on Higher Education, and as a member of the National Commission for UNESCO.

With this background, Dr. Tead's selection of a topic for the John Dewey Society Lecture was an especially happy one, and one that was more than timely. In the public discussion of eduction in recent years, higher education has been receiving an increasing amount of attention. On no other level of education, probably, have the issues been more starkly stated or the cleavages of points of view more sharply cut. And the discussion of no other level of education has received so dramatic an impetus as that given to the question of the training of scientists and technologists by the placing of the Russian sputniks in orbit. Some of the public discussion of higher education during the post-sputnik era has been constructive and significant. But too much of it has been ill-considered. Too many of the proposals for changes in higher education have been made almost thoughtlessly and without any real knowledge of the problems of higher education or any reasoned conception of the role it could and should play in a democratic system of schools. As a consequence, the total effect has often been one of confusion and contradiction, not to say hysteria.

In contrast with this atmosphere, Dr. Tead's lecture constitutes a calm and perceptive proposal. It is an attempt at a sound design for higher education. It is based on a thorough knowledge of the field. It presents a consistent conception of the nature and function of higher education. It is comprehensive in scope and discusses the implications of the proposal for all aspects of the institutional operation of higher education. It is a discussion which merits careful consideration. The John Dewey Society is honored to present this volume as the first of its Lectureship Series.

Preface

I am grateful to the John Dewey Society for the opportunity to present this lecture and make it available in print to a wider audience. And I am sensible of the great honor accorded me in becoming the first holder of this lectureship.

My choice of subject was animated by the prevailing sense of educational urgency and the oncoming pressures of larger college enrollments. It was also prompted by the desire to register a plea that quality of performance be stressed more consistently on more campuses as the numerical pressures mount, and as complacency of necessity gives way to questions about the inwardness and issues of teaching and learning.

This lecture is deliberately practical. It draws upon my own administrative experience in a number of institutions and my close contacts with several colleges in which learning is in central focus and results are heartening. The program elaborated here derives largely from the successful experience of these colleges. For they have made students want to learn because the climate is geared to the good of learning.

There is a price to pay for getting a better educational job done in American colleges. And I shall try to spell out the crucial odds in ways to encourage its payment.

I have written much elsewhere about what is to be mastered in the learning effort and hope to return to the theme in the future. In this lecture the focus is on the means to achieve the greatest stimulus to learning and only by indirection on the ultimate ends of education. For whatever immediate or long-range issues arise out of present tensions in higher education, we will have to keep our eyes always on good learning experiences as the central condition for intellectual mastery in college. Only at that point can we begin to formulate objectives.

My own concrete experience has brought me to focus on the single question: Is the student truly learning and if not how shall this be brought to pass?

This question, which I shall try to answer here, is not obsessive with me. It is at the core of our national dilemma. "What went ye out to seek?" is what we must ask today. And our answer must be: We seek in our colleges and universities the message of the wise and learned to the young and eager as to how the waste places are to be made fertile and the material goods are to be made to contribute to spiritual virtues. This is symbolic language. But the intent of the American college is transcendent in its nobility.

Obviously, only a fraction of this book was presented at the public lecture in Chicago on February 21, 1958, before the John Dewey Society. I was allowed the privilege of expanding my theme and offering a statement more than twice the length of the verbal presentation.

New York City   ORDWAY TEAD

The Climate
of Learning

FANTASY AND REALITY

There is no mystery about how to run a college to maximize student learning. There have been numerous examples of devotion to this major goal. There can be far more in the future. Indeed, there must be if the public expectancy about the process and product of higher education is to be realized at a justifiable level.

Imagine what it would be like to visit student lounges, eating halls, fraternities and sororities, eager student bull sessions, absorbed groups at faculty club lunch tables, and in all these places to hear spontaneous, informed, purposeful conversation on issues in some timely field—discussed with earnestness, intellectual grasp and competence. Imagine professors and students in their groups—specialists in disparate fields—discoursing intelligibly together on interdisciplinary themes. Imagine, also, this situation pervading not one campus but most campuses—in the undergraduate schools of universities, in liberal arts colleges, teachers' colleges, two-year colleges, up and down our land.

Our credulity may be taxed by these fantasies. But our incredulity might be the measure of the criticism currently levelled against colleges as failing to be places pervaded by impassioned, broadening, and contagious learning. Nor should such imagined changes suggest the introduction into education of self-conscious intellectual posturing. Surely it is one thing to have a sustained interest in the life of the mind, along with the natural prompting to sharpen one's wits with one's peers; it would be something else again if it were a pedantic straining for learned effect.

Certain shortcomings are matters of common knowledge and concern. One bit of critical documentation from the conclusions of the report by Professor Philip E. Jacob of the University of Pennsylvania suggests the extent to which college study has failed in altering students' schemes of values in the social science fields. His summary findings say:*

This study has not discerned significant changes in student values which can be attributed directly either to the character of the curriculum or to the basic courses in social sciences which students take as part of their general education.

This study has discovered no specific curricular pattern of general education, no model syllabus for a basic social science course, no pedigree of instructor and no wizardry of instructional method which should be patented for its impact on the values of students. Student values do change to some extent in college. With some students, the change is substantial. *But the impetus to change does not come primarily from the formal educational process. Potency to affect student values is found in the distinctive climate of a few institutions,* the individual and personal magnetism of a sensitive teacher with strong value-commitments of his own, or value-laden personal experiences of students imagina-

* See *Changing Values in College* by Philip E. Jacob (New York: Harper & Brothers, 1957), pp. 1-11.

tively integrated with their intellectual development. (Italics mine—O.T.)

I assume that if there has been such a signal failure to alter and improve social values, this failure has extended more generally to *other* areas of college and university purpose. For where learning has occurred to good effect, *all* learning has necessarily been advanced in desirable ways, and vice versa, since the two are inextricably combined.

The findings of the Jacob report reveal one major deviation from the norm.

"Similar as the patterns of student values appear on a mass view, the intellectual, cultural or moral 'climate' of some institutions stands out from the crowd. The response of students to education within the atmosphere of these institutions is strikingly different from the national pattern."

It is this favorable "climate" that I propose to examine and characterize. For the climate of learning is more than a phrase; it identifies the combined conditions in a college which arouse the desires of students to learn widely and deeply.

A different way of offering comparable evidence is found in the following quotation from a mimeographed memorandum on "The Nature of the College Community," published by the Fund for the Advancement of Education (November 13, 1956):

As to whether the campus community does in fact affect learning, a study made at Vassar was cited which noted that a distinguishable "student culture," with all the sociological implications of the word, does exist and the primary aim of the students is to be assimilated into that culture. Its effect tends to be a levelling one—pushing the reluctant learners and blunting the eager ones; the intellectual aims of the college are conditioned by this culture and become a part of it. To raise the intellectual culture we must raise the student culture.

This quotation stresses the learning difficulties arising from a separation of the college community into two camps of divergent cultures—the culture of the faculty and that of the students. It suggests the need for an effort to unify the two cultures.

❧

WHY FOCUS ON LEARNING?

First is the problem of increased enrollments. With the prospect of larger numbers of undergraduates, the result of the college outlay of time and money must be as productive as possible in individual student growth; also the teacher must multiply his or her influence to the possible maximum.

Second is a heightened popular expectancy that something worthwhile will accrue to student and to community out of the present college process. The promise has to be fulfilled alike in public and private institutions. This calls for the assurance of more and better learning, even though many may still find it hard to describe clearly the nature of the learning outcome they expect. On this score, educational leadership should surely be prepared to state within broad limits but in reasonably specific terms what the desirable objectives are and how they are to be attained.

Third, there is the factor of an internationally competitive educational condition to which we cannot shut our eyes.

A good solid education, not only in science and engineering but also in the total intellectual and moral equipment necessary for the responsible, affirmative, and imaginative citizen in a democracy, is required of more and more young people in any nation which like ours proposes to hold its eminent place in the world community.

Fourth, there is the likelihood that mastery of learning motives and methods by teachers and students alike can result in the same teacher guiding more students in more studies, with greater student independence and self-propulsion than is typical today.

❧

HOW ACHIEVE BETTER LEARNING

What are the environing influences that are conducive to improved student learning and zeal for learning? How are the college institutional philosophy and physical surroundings to be structured so as to encourage student learning motives and results?

The solution of this urgent problem of more sharply defined and more vigorously affirmed college objectives does not require a flight into fancy. Most if not all of the features of a positive program now operate in varying combinations in a number of institutions. We have heartening examples, and it is significant that they tend to be in the smaller, private institutions. Loving solicitude has not been absent here; it has favored an inventiveness, an open-minded flexibility, from which many other colleges should now profit as rapidly as possible. That the programs of colleges which have reexamined and reconstructed their educational policies in recent years are identical in no two cases is itself a gratifying index of the possibilities of experiment.

The primary lack has not been in ideas about programming. The lack, if I read the evidence aright, is in the *leadership to press these learning objectives* with persuasion and courage. This statement may seem surprising to those unacquainted with the campus world; for it is presumed that the purpose of higher education is to educate. This assumption, however, may be naive.

On too many campuses many responsible members of the faculty may know the objectives that they individually are striving to advance, but if asked about the *institutional objectives,* they would be hard put to it to give a commonly shared and cogent answer—an answer clearly consistent with the realities of sound campus life and purpose.

If it is suggested that the leadership necessary to assure the proper emphasis on learning is the responsibility of the college president, it should be remembered that the average tenure of the American college president is only four or five years. This is not a long enough period for one person, no matter how powerful his position or how persuasive his personality, to start and sustain a program in which the climate of learning will steadily improve and become increasingly indigenous.

Out of the confusion and inconsistency about over-all college aims there flow inevitable and familiar results. Of these some well-attested consequences are: that too many young people go to college for the wrong reasons; that entering students find themselves lonely, poorly guided, intellectually unequipped and unmotivated; that the process of learning is not made inviting or meaningful to them because faculty members are ill-informed on how to apply the psychology of learning; that standards of marks and promotions are either too hard, too easy, or inflexible and arbitrary; that the "side shows" of athletics and social activities take over the center of the stage and academic learning is slighted if not belittled as either bad form or merely necessary compensation for the enjoyment of "college life."

If leadership is a focal factor here, and if presidential leadership seems—statistically—to be precarious, in what directions do we look? Either the conditions which bring about a short presidential term have to be changed; or the president should give his firm support for a program in which leadership is assigned to the academic dean or similar officer. Someone on each campus has from now on to be charged unmistakably with dynamic, realistic responsibility for advancing the college's educational policy and program. This can perhaps not be expected of the president in any case in respect to a university's undergraduate colleges. And if the problems of financial and property administration are today preempting the time of many college presidents, that is one more reason why the college climate is unsatisfactory.

Rescue the college leadership to its rightful educational role! This is an urgent demand upon legislators, trustees, and faculties. The appointment of top-ranking executives in charge of development (money-raising), public relations, buildings and grounds, and new construction—a functional centralization—is essential if the increasingly serious burden of quality education is to be assumed aggressively by one individual focused upon giving the lead to more and better learning.

Improvement of the climate of learning is thus in most institutions dependent initially upon a reconstituted administrative structure. If first things in the college are to be put first *and kept first,* a firm, courageous, intellectually wide-ranging leader of learning must be on the job.

❧

THE NEED FOR
SIGNIFICANT LEARNING

Prefatory to any program of measures to change the climate and to upgrade the student culture has surely to be a more widespread grasp among faculty members of *what constitutes significant learning.* Indeed students themselves should also be made aware early in the college years of what it is *they* should expect from their learning as well as the ways of carrying it on effectively. Reference can be made here only to a few books in the growing body of explanatory literature on this subject.* Such reference is essential because many professorial individuals will rise up to affirm that there is little question but that their students are getting good marks and therefore learning well. This defensive response to the kind of criticism that needs to be made represents traditional views of traditional methods in securing traditional results. These are no longer sufficient.

Enough is known of typical weaknesses and of methods to

* See Delmar M. Goode, *These Books Were Stimulating* (Oregon State College, 1955).

help toward a new reorientation even though all the theoretical answers are not yet in. One reads with sympathy, for example, the testimony of Professor Tilton of Yale, from the field of educational psychology, when he says:

We would find considerable agreement, I think, that the educational task is psychologically very complex, invoking to an important degree the development of memory, perception, meaning, understanding, intelligence, transfer, problem solving, interests, attitudes, appreciations, values, and ideals, as well as the development of habits and skills.*

With this cautionary prelude let us see if present knowledge to which Dewey contributed so richly has not more to offer.

❧

KINDS OF LEARNING PATTERNS

It is the relatively passive role which the student has usually been asked to play that prompts the most insistent criticism of learning theory. The student listens to lectures on a schedule, he reads from required readings, he memorizes what students guess will be asked on examination papers. The ideas and concepts handled are often what Whitehead called "inert," irrelevant to student experience and concern. The student goes through the motions because the traditional situation forces this upon him.

The vacuity of all this, the folly of conceiving it as learning in any true sense, is realized when one contrasts the

* See lecture by J. W. Tilton, *Frontiers of Education* (Phila., Pa.: University of Pennsylvania Press, 1957), p. 39.

methods, motives, and results with those of professional education. The analogy is informing even though it shows much college teaching in a withering light. In a law school the student studies both principles and examples (cases) of the legal matters about which he as a lawyer will be consulted. He puts this knowledge to the trial test in a "moot court." He is usually keenly motivated from within by drives that lead to intensive and rewarding application to the tasks assigned. The learning here exemplifies self-drive toward competence in a self-chosen activity with self-satisfying as well as socially approved results.

The college athletic coach—to offer another illustration—has at his best to be an expert teacher because he seeks to have every player develop self-drive toward competence in his sport with outcomes gratifying to himself and to the college community. Indeed a whole lecture could be elaborated for the edification of professors as to the several strategies by which the coach systematically builds a conditioning milieu and supporting structure focused on football-learning and football-winning. Much classroom motivation looks paltry in any comparison with what is required in the austerity, hard work, and *imagination* of the regimen employed to turn out a winning team.

❧

LEARNING ANALYZED

The teacher in turn should have the expectation of some valuable permanent *difference* in student learning responses in point of attitude and conduct, direct and indirect, present and future, conscious and unconscious, specific and general. These differences are the evidences that learning has truly occurred. There has to be the immediate or prospective *use* of what is learned in areas of thought, feeling, and act—not necessarily in a utilitarian or vocational sense, but as integrated into the whole person as a new resource with which to confront the variegated life situations that are destined to arise.

Indeed since it is always the whole person who is learning as each new acquisition yields its nourishment, the present sharply conceived distinction between different kinds of learning should be recognized as a false dichotomy. Learning for some overt instrumental purpose, often vocational, and learning for its own sake, or to satisfy curiosity, or for cultural enrichment, cannot be separated. The uses of one's learnings are not foreseeable nor are they all "practical" in the usual meaning of that word.

On the other hand, there is learning which is by memorization—foreign language vocabularies, scientific formulae, or other essential factual data. These need the directive supplied by the good teacher, assuring the student's explicit knowledge of the connection of the facts with the subject and the connection of the subject and its facts with the student.

But the response of the learner to any specific learning process should early in the process give rise to some sense of imputed value for *him*. If the student feels that no value or benefits accrue, his effort to assimilate a particular offering of learning will lose zest. This fact points to the truth that it is impossible to separate knowledge and values; too, there is an emotional experience with acquiring new knowledge that is itself a valuing experience. Knowing and valuing are in reality two facets of all learning processes, and one trouble with some college pedagogy is that it centers on the accumulative and ignores the affective aspects of learning. The teacher has to concern himself with *how the student feels about* what is offered to be learned. If the feeling is negative, the learning will be negligible.

The motivations to learning have constantly to be stressed if the climate of learning is to be fair and warm. The desirable end is a self-starting, self-propelling eagerness for more learning as helpful to a more abundant and intelligent responsiveness to the individual's life encounters. The self-improvement resulting from more and better learning will naturally range over wide fields of activities and diverse channels of expression. Learning is essentially toward richer selfhood, but the directions taken can vary widely from the self-centered to the self-transcendent.

This doctrine is not novel but it takes patience to get it into the bloodstream of the colleges. A corroborative view from an authoritative source is well set forth as follows:

Increase in the responsibilities of students should extend to their own consciously planned learning. Students should require less detailed direction of their study and should be thrown more upon their own responsibilities. Some observers believe that, in comparison with students in other parts of the world, American students are often spoon-fed by a lecture and a course-examination system inappropriate in many ways to their maturity. A system in which increased responsibility for learning is thrown on the individual student should be developed, adequately safeguarded by a counseling and consultative program. There should be more planned student discussions, more individual exploration of intellectual interests, less reliance upon detailed supervision from instructors, more effort to appraise and credit growth resulting from a student's own initiative.*

With the prospect of more students per teacher, and with the practical mandate that each student should continue into adult life his drive to acquire a larger body of operational knowledge as well as to handle his leisure with productive resourcefulness, this problem of self-motivation assumes greater importance than ever. Colleges have a grave responsibility to oversee the intellectual life and cultivate the learning skills of their students so that they will learn to enjoy the habits of the life of the mind and reap the satisfactions of its progressive pursuit.

When the learning which the college teacher calls for has its own intrinsic appeal of rational, esthetic, or spiritual usefulness in the broadest sense, the prospects are that in *learning to learn,* the student is also hopefully learning to *like* to learn. As a college objective the strengthening of this desire needs more explicit focus and more demonstration of its personal rewards. Happily we are here involved with desires that grow in strength with what they feed upon.

Self-motivation is thus necessarily at the center of concern here. And this means—to recapitulate—that each student's mind and feelings are being led to discover in the matter studied a challenging, absorbing, usable mentally focused experience, developing as his study proceeds. Responsibility for achieving this desirable end is a dual one. The teacher has to present his subject as humanly related in thought and feel-

* See "Higher Education in a Decade of Decision," Educational Policies Commission, N.E.A., Washington, D.C., 1957, p. 54.

ing; the student has to come to see it as related to *him*. Its relation to him can be due to various appeals but the experiences have sooner or later to prove rewarding enough to prompt continuance of the effort.

❦

LEARNING SKILL
AS A PARTIAL OBJECTIVE

One further word about learning in this context has to do with the relation which should be clarified and strengthened toward upholding the desirable broad college objectives and purposes which are specifically centered on the learning experience itself.

Subject matter is always learned in the course of learning to learn and liking to learn. But my own emphasis is instrumental, because of my conviction that a myopia prevails among college teachers about the learning effort as an intrinsic process. Policy and program at the thought-process level of concern are primary to good college teaching. The world of teachers and students, however, has not yet wholly caught up with this truth and its operational implications. Concretely, John Dewey's classic, *How We Think,* first published in 1909, and other volumes for example, Arthur E. Murphy's *The Uses of Reason* and Edwin Arthur Burtt's *Right Thinking,* suggest areas in which competence has to be consciously sought and realized by all concerned.

This is not to imply any neglect of imparting subject-matter; it is rather to stress a prior intellectual condition in the teacher's strategy in handling his material so that it appeals to and stays with the student as meaningful to him.

Once this consciousness of the way the mind acquires knowledge becomes firmly ingrained, the student will consciously strengthen the drive to *continue* with lively, responsive uses of the mind in subsequent experience and with *all* problems confronted. *To learn to want to keep on learning is one of the priceless assets of the right kind of collegiate experience.* This conscious outreaching has also to include the needful aspect of knowing how to go about looking for the knowledge pertinent to one's many-sided questionings.

College learning includes a variety of fringe, "halo," or indirect results to which the wise teacher will give attention as study proceeds. Indirect and by-product learnings can occasionally yield the finest values. I refer here to esthetic appreciative power; skill in oral and written communication; some life outlook or philosophy which helps to integrate and give spiritual substance to one's career; a capacity for affection that yields consideration and compassion in human relations; a sense for sharing in social relations to the extent that one assumes some productive degree of civic and economic responsibility; awareness of an example of rectitude, or nobility of character that stirs one to emulation.

It is perhaps too extreme to say that if learning in most of these collateral directions has not been deeply and permanently achieved in college, the over-all program has failed. The usual alternative is to say (defensively) that the curriculum has been contrived to be subject-centered. And where this is true, students are often so overburdened with the particularities of each of their five courses, that the generalized residual learnings, which much college instruction should really be at pains to impart, get lost. The subject matter itself is then usually forgotten in short order, and the significant learning gain has been virtually nil.

We know the familiar quip that college education is that which remains after we have forgotten what we have learned. To me, it is a damning indictment of the ineffectual unawareness colleges tend to have for the inwardness, the *personalness*, of the learning effort. The truer, and psychologically more valid, aphorism would be that college education comprises those altered attitudes, habits, and loyalties which become built-in to the learning person because of the college experience. College is to forward knowledge, skills, and feelings that yield a capacity to cope with life with zest, goodwill, reason, and growing awareness.

If those responsible for shaping the content of college education do not know what they want to see learned, what personal qualities they expect the growth process to include, and what kind of adults, with what kinds of competences, they would like to be able to point to with pride in their alumni, they will never get far in organizing a unified program to assure genuine learning.

❦

DRAWING ON PRESENT EXAMPLES

I come now to an enumeration of some essential particulars of a program structured to improve the climate of learning. You may object that my items are too all-embracing and thus, in some degree, indirect or remote in influence; or that factors are cited which are too trivial or beyond control to command into action.

Or you may protest that this becomes a lecture on how to run a college with most programmatic aspects briefly alluded to, many of which are already matters of customary operating concern. Indeed some may say that the procedures can be taken for granted as present. All such objections have plausibility. But I ask the student of learning to hear me through with suspended judgment since it is an entire strategy I would like to advance as one unified program.

My selection of items of method is offered in the light of successful experience in one or another institution. Also, there will be those colleges in which permeative not to say revolutionary influences will have to be injected if this desirable improvement in climate is eventually to occur.

Some of these program items will, of course, be found easier to adopt in one institution, and others in another. The fact is, however, that every plank in the following platform is matched by successful practice in several institutions. And if an excess of wishful idealism or expectation is imputed to my program, my plea is, guilty!

❧

THE NEED FOR LEADERSHIP

I have already stressed as a primary requirement an enthusiastic *leadership* to assure a vigorous and inspiriting campus climate. Real obstacles stand in the way of such indispensable leadership. But, practically speaking, if the president of the college will initiate the program and give it emphatic moral support, and if an academic dean who commands the respect and regard of faculty and students is chosen to spearhead it, it should be possible to get the program off the ground and into gradual operation.

There is not space here to elaborate on the tactics of persuasion necessary to assure all the needed advances. Every college administrator knows that there will be resistance on the part of various vested interests all along the line. These can be of several kinds—faculty complacency, student traditions, alumni memories. Fearfulness and inertia on the campus in the face of possible change are powerful obstacles. Perhaps the adroit tactic is to persuade each vested interest that its group is likely to be benefited by some element in the program of improving the climate of learning.

The truth is that experience with beneficial outcome is contagious. Yet on the other hand the preliminary reaction —whether of faculty, student, or trustee groups—is often dubious and even flatly hostile. For example, alumni at an early point may close in and loudly contend that under new and more austere academic standards their sons may not qualify to enter college, and also that its football eminence and their loyalty to it will be threatened. Older faculty members, moreover, often become exasperated at having to revise one or another classroom routine including their dog-eared lecture notes.

❧

THE ROLE OF THE TRUSTEES

This situation means in administrative language that, given a good educational leader, the trustees must be chosen and be educated to be behind a strong program of serious application to intensive learning effort. For the threatening repercussions of proposed alterations can spread to loyal trustees with an unerring and disruptive speed. And alumni and their trustee spokesmen have, therefore, to be made to realize that an institution has to pay the price for adhering with integrity to any self-consistent, strongly focused and rigorous educational program.

It would seem axiomatic that the legally responsible body in any educational organization would have some clear vision of the objectives which it is sworn to serve, and would pronounce in support of such proposed policies as are required in the premises. But this axiom, oddly enough, is not universally in effect.

Get in tune with your college's objectives. Have the right objectives to be loyal to. These are dicta that should have initial application to trustees. But beyond this the same doctrine applies equally to faculties, and also to the students themselves for the good reason that students can in reality modify, dilute, or nullify educational purposes. The fact is that only what students decide to accept as operational does in fact become operative.

I leave this important mention of the trustees with the admonition that without their sympathetic backing the failure of a "tough" program may be preordained.

❧

THE FACULTY'S ROLE

This brings us to the faculty and the requirement of support from a substantial majority of its members—wholehearted and informed as to the reasons for and methods of the program advocated. Practically, this will arouse different resistances in the college of a university from those in an individual college. But the basic needs are similar. Incoming teachers in both situations have to be chosen for the right reasons—deliberately aimed at advancing freshman student learning in psychologically valid ways. Beyond scholarly competence, college teachers must have a deep interest in the importance of the *process* of education as eager learning, and a friendly concern for the student as a young adult in his or her formative stages. The kind of teaching first-year students experience saves them for or drives them from a scholarly career. Give the freshmen your best teachers and implicate them emotionally in the glamour of a learning career. This is the second wise strategy in a program to improve the climate of learning.

"Character," said Emerson, "teaches over our heads"— a maxim that needs to be blazoned prominently in the offices of presidents, deans, and department heads as they interview prospective teachers. For here is where the direct, the concrete exhibits of learning as embodied in persons are to be beheld by the student. Does learning thus embodied appear inherently dull, unattractive, and unimpressive? Or is there some phosphorescence, some exciting quality that weds beguiling intellectual superiority to an appealing though tempered worldliness?

It is in the light of such factors that student attitudes toward learning are molded and faculty personalities appraised as to their loyalty to learning objectives. This is assuredly true in the student's first two impressionable years of exposure to what may be his initial encounter with someone professionally concerned with the life of the mind. If the faculty examples reveal warped or disturbed personalities, students will not respond, contribute to or profit from the climate we are seeking.

The selection of teachers is thus perhaps the single most important responsibility of the entire college administration. It conditions every aspect of the educational offensive, for it is continuously involved in shaping the student response toward productive learning.

❦

THE SELECTION OF STUDENTS

The next item in a forward-looking program is the right choice of students. But let it not be surmised that I favor selecting students only from the top I.Q.'s. It is relatively easy to run a college of high test students, who tend to have self-conscious, prideful motives for self-advancement. The challenge of securing truly enthusiastic self-propulsion toward academic effort is rather to be found most among the far larger proportion of young people with I.Q.'s from 100 to 125. The problem of intellectual mastery among these students is resolved by their efforts to achieve maximum use of the varied powers that they may have, rather than by efforts that are purely and solely academic.

As we look ahead to the college of a decade hence, we may discover that some modification is necessary in the meaning usually assigned to such phrases as "academic learning" and "academic attainment."

There are different kinds of minds. They are multidimensional; in addition to those high in verbal conceptual talents, there is a preponderance of others that have to be ministered to, nourished, and disciplined in a broadened academic frame. In college (as in the population at large) a variety of mental aptitude patterns exist, including those of the verbal generalizer, the engineer, the scientific researcher, the esthete, the extreme extrovert in human relations, the professional person of varied proclivities in law, medicine, ministry, and teaching, as well as some few who seem to have no markedly special bent at all.

Given the modest mental endowment of about 105 I.Q., all of these types of persons can gain much from the right kind of college under well-structured total learning auspices. What they consciously experience of the prevailing sentiment or student community culture is determinative in shaping more mature attitudes toward their learning. And this pattern of instruction includes not only "book learning" in the conventional sense but activities that bring into play the less bookish and more "performing" occasions of learning. Ingenuity in the use of discussion, debate, case analysis, role playing, visual aids, class reports, and any other contrivances will be essential in order to have the class experience learning on other than a purely abstruse and conceptualized level. Also the student must be consciously encouraged to participate in congenial co-curricular activities that supplement and give expression to talents that are not always taken account of in the classroom. Verbal abstractive capacity cannot and should not be thinned down nor can the need to memorize essential information be ignored. But both of these requirements have to be used in relation to the total learning outlook and aptitude of the student.

DISTURBING FACTORS

With respect to productive student learning, a word should be said about assuring wholesome emotional adjustment as helping to condition attentiveness to learning. There is today abundant evidence that an unpredictable minority of incoming students will be mentally disturbed to the point of having their learning interest or ability temporarily impaired or distracted. This takes form in feelings of insecurity, inferiority, fearfulness, and anxiety about social status and inability to measure up intellectually. The impact of disturbances at home, including the adverse effects of a broken home, can be severe. Many young people readily weather these storms incident to transition into college; but enough will suffer a real blockage or resistance to need positive help, including professional counseling services. The early identification of deeply distressed students is not easy; the skilled counseling resources of the college should be involved, with the house mothers, teachers, advisors, and fellow-students, all alert for intimations of trouble. Emotionally disturbed individuals can readily become focal points of student disaffection and restlessness of a most invidious kind unless they are promptly helped.

Financial worries including the difficulties incident to the pursuit of part-time work can be a serious deterrent to learning. Despite numerous and appealing instances of sacrifice and overwork enabling a student to stay in college, such students should usually be guided to take a longer time for their college course or to defer entering until they have more cash in hand. Unless the timing of each student's activities can include enough leisure occasionally to think things over and to assimilate what is being studied in free and unrestrained companionship with one's peers, a valuable asset of college, as well as a stimulus to learning, is irretrievably lost.

On the positive side, students who fit into the college regimen with little or no resistance can become centers of courage and competence, and examples of a successful attack on learning. Their aid in morale-building should be consciously enlisted by an alert administration.

An instance of the special case which is now becoming less special is the enrollment of married undergraduates who wish to live as a family on or near the campus. Testimony is unanimous in finding such students enjoying a superior motivation, application, and academic record. This situation may well suggest that our present pattern of rigidly fixed four secondary years followed at once by four college years is not absolutely wise or sacred. Indeed, it might be well to encourage more participation in the college experience *after* a break of years and a return when wholesome motives for learning have been aroused by the maturing impact of life's experience. The G.I. Bill of Rights' students supplied abundant evidence of the truth of the benefits of this flexibility in timing.

❦

THE IMPORTANCE OF GUIDANCE

A supporting feature the need for which has grown by leaps in the last two decades is the provision of an adequate guidance staff to offer counsel to students on various questions. With the increasing numbers of students it is no longer realistic to assume that their individual relation to all aspects of college operation will proceed smoothly and to their own best educational advantage.

There is a pressing demand for advice about a wide variety of problems. Among these are questions about the initial selection of courses as well as their programming through the four years, including the choice of a major; about social adjustments in their several aspects, together with possible family maladjustments; about financial burdens, including necessary help as to summer work and post-college employment; and about the unsettlements of faith, distorted philosophies of life, and spiritual confusion.

A comprehensive counseling program, with guidance personnel integrated as closely as possible with the instructional staff and the curricular process, constitutes a major, *essential* adjunct of any systematic effort to have students come to terms with an aggressive learning program. If there is intelligent solicitude about all the forces that can shape student motives toward good educational application, the learning prospects are advanced by so much, since inhibiting obstacles are thus consciously faced and minimized. Only with humane, wise, and comprehensive guidance will this learning objective be obtainable today and tomorrow.

The whole range of advisory services has now reached virtually professional proportions. But as this professionalization becomes more intensive it will be important to assure that the human touch of the counselor is not lost. Professionalism has the inherent danger that its ends tend to obscure or eclipse the ends of a dedicated ministry to troubled minds and souls. And student advisory workers have always to be conscious of this threat.

A special word is merited as to the need for intensive guidance with the many who are untrained in fruitful study methods. With approximately one-half of the students dropping out during high school and a like proportion not remaining to finish college, I am certain that ineffectual study habits are a potent contributing cause. There is a growing body of competent guides and aids on how to study and the essence of what is in these manuals should be clearly in the heads of all students if enormous amounts of time, energy, and goodwill are not to be lost by fumbling and inept efforts. The freshman orientation program becomes yearly more integral to good outcomes.

❦

COLLEGE EMPLOYMENT POLICIES

A neglected if secondary factor in building the learning climate is attention to the quality and attitude of the ancillary college personnel staff, who perform a wide variety of duties, who touch and affect the student directly and indirectly, and who teach students by example, often as effectively as formally appointed instructors.

A university is not a business organization (palpable evidence to the contrary notwithstanding). And the standards of staff requirements in terms of quality of personality should not be the same as those in business. Such standards should properly stress qualities of good personal and human approach, address, sympathy, and empathy. Student contacts include dealings with the admissions office, the bursar, the house and ground workers including (importantly in crisis) the campus police, the dormitory residence heads, the health officers, and those guidance officers who are not also met in the course of regular classroom teaching assignments.

The position is sound that in order to qualify all such workers should be consciously attuned to the educational motives and aims of the institution. Does this or that practice advance situations and relations in which educational ends are primary? Does the student become aware that he is the beneficiary of numerous facilitating services offered to help advance his learning through his association with the academic bureaucracy?

These are questions that need to be posed periodically by the responsible authorities as a matter of staff training. For the record is by no means universally satisfactory. Almost every campus can point to some one or more contact posts that are staffed by autocratic, impersonal, routine-bound aids to whom students are a nuisance, albeit a necessary element in their day's work. Were a modern personnel policy to supervene in the hiring, training, and retiring of this personnel, a marked improvement in student morale might result on many campuses. The slogan here might well be: we hire only and always those who will complement the educational process.

❧

ADEQUATE MAINTENANCE
OF PROPERTY

This philosophy of facilitation and planned support requires that the entire physical property be thought of as designed to lend every possible aid and comfort to education and to contribute to a climate favorable to wholesome learning. This is a wide-ranging mandate of administrative responsibility.

Periodic coverage of property maintenance by careful check lists should be introduced in institutions large and small in order to replace feeble maintenance measures and casual inspections. I need only mention the problems of fire, of noise, of provisions for smoking, of adequate, quiet study space, of adequate library reading space, of social rooms which will include provisions for social life between the sexes. Many colleges are seriously short of space set aside solely for concentrated study.

Common sense suggests that dormitory units should not be too large, and some provisions of "houses," "colleges," or fraternity-leased accommodations—all looking to decentralized living—are surely to be preferred to assure personalized and humanly containable living and learning units.

Special consideration should be given to the animating spirit and atmosphere of the college library. The librarians are crucial people in implementing the pursuit of learning. Their helpfulness and solicitude can make the library a prime resource both for immediate learning purposes and for the student's lifelong use of this most civilized instrument of man's culture.

I shall be told that the student who wants to study will somehow find a place to study—which may be broadly true. But the problem is to create for the unaroused, the neutral, and the slow student congenial surroundings that inspire and help him to concentrate upon study. The invitation to learning is in all common sense also the invitation to be able to share in the physical supports that can minister to the desire to learn, of which ample quiet study areas are of primary importance.

❦

THE ROLE OF THE CURRICULUM

The climate of learning is strengthened if the whole structure of the curriculum is designed to challenge student curiosity, invite student problem-solving, and relate major studies to subsequent vocational or professional prospects and other basic life interests. That a desire to learn can be evoked by a thoughtfully conceived and reconstructed curriculum is not a matter of conjecture. The literature describing the beneficial effect on students is reassuring as is the consensus of testimony from all other sources.

The claims and needs of true learning are not incompatible with a liberal program or purpose. The phrase, "general education," for example, is used increasingly to identify the newer programs as distinguished from the term, "liberal education"; yet a careful examination reveals little difference in basic objectives. The difference is mainly one of strategy. And that strategy is in harmony with the point of view presented here— namely, a clear *relating* in the presentation of college subjects to student intellectual outlook and responsiveness as it will, with the proper stimulus, reveal itself during the freshman year.

This means neither talking down to students nor any meritricious seeking out of dubious or spurious student "interests." It means rather pitching the classroom attack to the student level of knowledge, awakened interests, verbal competence, aptitudes, and problems. The purpose here is to motivate a growing self-drive toward sustained learning. General education would stress the relevance and the interrelationships to current life of the sciences, social studies, and humanities. Its aim of developing growth in understanding, intellectual skills, mature emotional and esthetic attitudes is a liberalizing aim.

An initial leverage to learning is whatever combination of intrinsic and extrinsic motives that proves compelling for the student in his search for self-mastery as the college instruction begins. Vocational interests should of course be enlisted as they arise and are found a pertinent and powerful motivation in the individual's studies.

To have the student reap as soon as possible the rewards of greater awareness and understanding, of greater grasp and command, is to quicken his curiosity and tax his powers of application to the maximum. These are the ways in which his learning comes to be self-regarding. Desirable habits of concentration can gain root and should be an objective in freshman year; and they will grow in strength as intellectual gratification is experienced increasingly in breadth and depth in the succeeding three years.

I anticipate that with larger enrollments curricular offerings will (and should) orient liberal and general subjects more explicitly toward their potential vocational application. If kept in proper perspective by wise teachers, this outlook will be a gain, not a limitation. At present the dividing line is too sharp, and the separatist attitude of professors too definite, between instruction that has liberal aims and instruction that has vocational aims. John Dewey was among the first to emphasize that all study could be at once disinterested, or liberal, and vocationally directed, *depending on how it is taught*. And liberal colleges have been deficient—not to say snobbish—in that their teachers have been reluctant to answer the tacit question of their students: What value may this or that course have in illuminating the occupation to which I look forward?

A flexible curriculum is enormously important in advancing deeper, broader learning experience. And it goes without saying that results depend upon its being served by a willing, convinced, and enthusiastic faculty. The introduction of curricular reforms in recent years has demonstrated the large amount of time, thought, interdepartmental collaboration, and periodic reevaluation of effort which these programs entail when they yield their best results. The central motive enlisting faculty devotion to such projects is the realistic admission on the part of a majority that the old ways did *not* produce learning of deep and permanent value. The teacher's honest self-examination, conjoined with study of the currently understood psychology of learning and the newer trends in curricular reform, should bring to bear motives for change leading to helpful and realistic alterations of subject organization and classroom techniques.

Experience has taught that under wise direction the various methods of encouraging independent study—broader reading, extended theses on major projects—lead to more sustained, thorough, and self-prompted learning effort than do the traditional lectures or recitations.

❦

THE USES OF TESTING

Much more can also be done with the improved use of tests, exams, and other forms of written check-up, if we would get away from memorized learning and other kinds of mere regurgitative checking. The last word of research has not been said on this subject; but until there is clearer evidence, the essay type of exam with questions carefully contrived to elicit *thought* answers and not memorized answers can help to encourage good learning attitudes. If the purpose of examinations is to determine the student's progress in bringing his rational powers to bear upon the subjects currently studied, improvements in examining techniques will inevitably result. I say this with full realization of the great progress in techniques of measurement being made most notably by the Educational Testing Service of Princeton, New Jersey. But they have done more with abilities, interests, aptitudes than with methods of subject-course marking.*

Indeed improvements in this direction should reduce the possibility of cheating on exams and thus perhaps indirectly lead to the restoration of honor systems in colleges which abandoned them because of administrative difficulties—notably the relative ease of cheating under traditional examining conditions and the reluctance of students to report the offenses of their classmates.

❧

ACCORDING ADEQUATE APPROVALS

A most important way of stimulating a healthy climate is through formalized approvals and honors, publicly acknowledged, for sound learning and high scholarship.

* See *Educational Testing Service*, Annual Report 1956-1957, Princeton, New Jersey.

I have mentioned the tutorial program, honors programs, and individual upperclass thesis requirements, all of which look to more independent and intensive relations of students to learning. Programs of which Swarthmore has supplied a pilot instance are now widely adopted as incentive devices and as public evidence of academic attainment. Another example is Harvard's new program to encourage more students earlier in their academic career to seek degrees with honors.

The dean's list is a valuable student-approval device if it is invested with an aura of serious achievement and is carefully selective. The same is true of all other honors attainments. The annual "honors day convocation" can be a most appealing way to accord public acknowledgment to academic mastery, as can public commencement recognition of learning achievements. Honors societies can be consciously cultivated; the Phi Beta Kappa and analogous honors groups in special fields have an important role in public approval programs.

Of similar benefit are inter-fraternity awards accorded annually to the fraternity or sorority which has the highest academic average among its members.

Sending of semester grades to parents and secondary school heads is a policy that aids indirectly by encouraging parental approbation for good work.

On the obverse side is the value of "watch lists" kept of borderline students, who, with judicious personal attention from teachers and advisors, can often be salvaged and even helped to eventual conspicuous attainment.

There is also much to be said for an annual award to the "teacher of the year" in recognition of outstanding teaching activity. Without doubt, pointing with pride to noteworthy teachers—as teachers not as scholars—can be a stimulus on the campus to improved concern about teaching skill that ministers to true learning.

❦

THE INTRODUCTION OF OUTSIDE SPEAKERS

Interest in learning can be further enhanced if care is taken that all speakers who appear on the campus are exemplars of wide learning and significant scholarship. Nothing can on occasion be more impressive and persuasive than a campus visitor as lecturer or consultant who is an unmistakable instance of "man thinking" with a rich and informed background. To show young people real intellectual achievement in action is always an incitement. It is that vision of greatness which Whitehead and before him, Emerson, wisely stressed. And whoever are in charge of chapels, assemblies, church services, subject-matter clubs and the like should be primed to seek such speakers to perform on campus platforms.

❦

THE VALUES OF CO-CURRICULAR LEARNING

It is an obvious thesis that the extra-curricular (recently better called the co-curricular) activities are positive educational forces. One reason, of course, why learning in these diverse areas is effective is that generally speaking they are self-selected by the student in line with self-recognized interests, aptitudes, and abilities. Here may well be one ideal learning situation.

The range of experiences in these self-chosen activities can be great and the learning benefits high. Indeed so valuable are these channels of learning that without it being too organizationally obvious, there should be deans of students, club advisors, and faculty consultants explicitly selected to stimulate, guide, and follow through on policy, activity, and enlistment.

I can only mention the intricate subject of student government. Its educational force as a stimulus to wholesome learning can be great. Indeed, there is much to be said for the Antioch College policy of a *college community government* in which the community is conceived as operating on a basis including faculty as well as students.

Subject-matter clubs, student publications, co-ed social events, dramatic and musical organizations—these are all vital areas of co-curricular experience and learning exposure. But they must be planned and clearly overseen by an administration which reenforces their educational value.

The educational value of athletics is all too often not appraised accurately or honestly by college administrators. If the question is asked: What may the student learn by the example of the complex and occasionally dubious strategies that enter into the conduct of intercollegiate sports, especially on a big-time basis? the answer is that the lessons to be learned are often by no means in harmony with much that is taught in the classroom or propounded by the religious exponents of the college. If the climate of learning is to be intensified and generalized on a high plane of ethical and moral convictions, the athletic picture has in its every aspect to be brought under the same critical evaluation. Hypocrisy and double talk bedevil the athletic scene today in too many institutions where big-time games and victory are the controlling end and where athletic activity is not regarded solely as an educational means to the individual student's physical development. Indeed, what students learn from today's intercollegiate sports programs is in need of brave and ethical reevaluation.

Other co-curricular activities that should be grouped under some administrative auspices are the various college service or welfare organizations—both those initiated by the students and those coming from the community that seeks to enlist the students. There is a splendid opportunity in most institutions to offer helpful, needed community services in which students under supervision are encouraged to volunteer their share to the advantage of the local agencies and with important learning opportunities for the students.

Since the study-work alternation programs (of which the University of Cincinnati is one of the oldest examples) are not likely to be put into early effect in all colleges, this community service program can go an appreciable way in getting students exposed to the local life and institutions in a realistic manner. They may thus minimize the town-gown separation, and ferti-lize by virtue of concrete contacts the more abstract learning experiences of the classroom.

❦

STUDENT-FACULTY RELATIONS

Social relations between faculty families and students can have great value if they are pursued in a natural, spontaneous way. Campus traditions on this score vary widely. Where this interchange has been at a minimum (restricted to apple-polishing), I am convinced that there is a loss of learning evocation. As an encouragement to this relationship a modest expense account could be offered by the college to faculty members to cover costs of entertaining—since food is a great social amalgam in such student gatherings!

Many will say that faculty contacts with students are satisfied by the classroom encounter—a view especially held valid in the larger universities. But surely if there is any virtue in a relationship with an older person, emulated for intellectual and other mature qualities and achievements, the college is the place where the right hand of fellowship can be extended from the admired scholar to the admiring neophyte. There is a fillip here for better student learning which is hard to assess at a high enough value.

Finally, there should be a balance preserved, by any one of several devices, to assure that no student carries more co-curricular activities than his energies and abilities can swing in competition with the formalized learning program—which is the primary concern.

❦

PROVIDING SPACE FOR STUDY

As I stated earlier, living and working accommodations are significant in lending physical aid to the act of studying, as well as in enhancing the symbolic dignity with which the effort to study is architecturally invested. There must be ample places conducive to study (some with smoking allowed) available from eight in the morning until midnight at least. And if such spaces do not exist, or if they are shabby, unattractive, or crowded, this is by way of the college saying to the students, "We defy you to study and learn under the physical space conditions we have provided."

My mention of poor study facilities is reiterated because from the student view it can be one of the major deterrents to a favorable climate of learning.

❧

STUDY-WORK ALTERNATIONS

A more controversial element in a program—but one which I advance with conviction—is the stimulus to richer learning by any one of the various forms of study-work interchange. Those, like myself, who agree with Professor Baker Brownell* about the artificial dissociation of college students from normal community living, creating a motivational vacuum and a delay in adult functioning, are always in search of a variety of means for keeping the student's personal roots firmly planted in some local community.

No intensive examination of programs and results of study-work programs is in order here. But no one can examine, even cursorily, the last two decades' experience of a score of colleges with variants of alternated study-work arrangements and not be impressed both with the growing vitality of the idea and with the splendid results. Special mention should be made of the manifest learning values, for example, of work-camp ex-

* See his *The College and the Community* (New York: Harper & Brothers, 1952), Chapter III.

periences as provided in a number of Friends (Quaker) projects; in the "year abroad" idea of some colleges; and in all the institutions which have capitalized on holiday or vacation field work arrangements with various kinds of employers. Indeed, so valuable is this extra-academic experience as a motivational spur that I foresee—and advocate—many more colleges going on a four-quarter plan in which one of the quarters each year is systematically devoted to required, directed off-campus field work.

The student's curiosity will be sparked by this non-curricular experience—which is new, interesting, and practical. It will liberate heretofore untapped powers, as with a race horse, eager to be released to run.

❧

IMPROVED RELATIONS WITH SECONDARY SCHOOLS

Recent experiments have given new point to the recommendation that all colleges work in closer conjunction with the secondary schools on ways of integrating curricular offerings and learning efforts. There are numerous good reasons for this in terms of an accentuation of learning interest especially focused on transition to the early college years. There is the value of careful selection of a college with closer knowledge of the applicant's mental aptitudes. There is the economy to be effected by not duplicating in a boring way in freshman year one or another high school studies. There is the opportunity to dramatize the change of teaching method as well as content to make an exciting distinction between the approaches of high school and of college work. There is the desirability of a formal program of testing freshmen in specified subjects to allow them to gain advanced standing either in individual courses (as in the languages) or in the entire program of first-year subjects. Indeed whatever devices will challenge the top capacity of every secondary senior and college freshman student are desirable aids to widening, deepening, and accelerating the learning effort. The evidence seems overwhelming that to thrust the secondary graduate into the new college situation up to the full extent of his abilities is a beneficial move.

So long as secondary schools are uneven in the quality of their instruction and standards, everything possible should be done in colleges to identify individual student ability and give it every chance at its own potential level of attainment without handicaps due to poor preparation. And let college and secondary educators stay close enough together in purpose and personal acquaintance to let the brilliant school student be offered advanced subject material sent down from the college he or she proposes to enter.

❦

LEVELING UP THE STUDENT CULTURE

It is next appropriate—indeed, crucial—to work toward unifying the cultures of the students and of the faculty. The goal is to create a better integrated community of learning, a more truly common intellectual outlook in substance and in goal, than is now typical. The intellectual and emotional separation of the generations is of course a fact and it is a critical fact not always adequately taken into account. Physical differences of age and divergent exposures to historic social experiences have to be reckoned with. But the effort to achieve a view of the world through a closer coincidence of angles of vision is not only possible, it is essential in the interest of academic vitality and relevance. We have to nurture the sympathetic feeling for intellectual kinship, which can so immensely further and deepen the learning effort. Students can realize its intrinsic appeal from their association with faculty members whose mental outlooks have retained their youthful cast.

It should, however, be appreciated that to close the gap between these two cultural climates requires solicitude initially from the *faculty* and administration. The overtures should properly come from the more mature segment of the academic community. And they have to be without condescension, without forced eagerness, but with a foundation of genuinely affectionate concern. Faculty members have to realize that they are not just trying to educate. There is always someone upon whom the education is focused. The verb to educate is here transitive; it requires an object. And the student groups are the important objects—younger human beings in search of maturity, willing to emulate, and eager to adventure.

Teachers should never forget that today's students were children during World War II, that World War I is to them ancient history, and that the big depression occurred before they were born. The claims of boy friends and girl friends, of social and athletic functions, and their week ends off campus, even the speed of air transportation to home or resort, contribute to an outlook on life on the part of the twenty-year-old quite different from that of typical faculty members.

If the sights of the two groups are to be helped to coincide more closely, there has to be heightened sensitivity, sympathy, and understanding among the older group. What will yield this is as much conscious intention as any other single factor. If the faculty members want to get their minds reasonably inside the minds and attitudes of the twenty-year-olds, let them start by *listening*. Then let them show that their life orientation is not "old fogy" but contemporary, aware, and *intellectually seasoned*.

This may lead, hopefully, a few steps in the direction of cultural unification. But the desirable result will also be the product of further procedures that faculties can study and apply. To point out the appeal of intellectual effort is a pioneering job with young people, despite the fact that *socially* they often seem as sophisticated as the faculty with whom they are associating. The intensified *human,* as contrasted with the institutional, contact of faculty with students is crucial to implementing our central purpose. Through faculty eyes education has to be always *con amore,* if it is to yield its richest fruits.

If the student self-image in its local cultural environment excludes the learning effort as unappealing or as bad form, the resistance to a more intellectual atmosphere will be correspondingly greater; and the whole effort will be retarded.

The common picture of the serious student as cloistered or monastic, as a "grind" and an "egghead," has to be offset by the obviously healthy, adjusted attitude of those who are the campus brains. Such an image can count immensely for strength once an upgrading of student attitude on this score is started. What has to become accepted is that college is a serious place, a genuinely challenging, indeed, an *exciting* place.

Similarly, in relation to the student self-image, there has to be put at rest the notion that the student as learner is in a sacrificial role and is denied the good things of life. With poor teaching, with teaching solely directed toward some ambiguous future applications, with teaching as trying to store knowledge into the compartments of the mind in the archaic empty-box analogy, learning can, of course, be a bleak and mirthless chore. But conceived as one of the avenues of self-fulfillment, it can yield the joy of awareness, of growth, and of mastery. Unless learning takes its place in the life of the individual as one of the major developmental mediums of self-release and self-actualization, it has not been given its full measure. And the self-image has remained a negative and unattractive one.

An affirmative self-image is well set forth by Professor Mark Van Doren* as follows:

The fruit of learning is that the person who has it enjoys his life, which is to say, the life of his mind, for that is the specifically human thing about him. The happy man has a good time with his mind. That is the end of education beyond which, surely, there is no other end. And it does not arrive for the student who has never had a happy teacher: one, that is, who had a good time with *his mind*. Happiness of this sort is infectious; it can even be epidemic. But let us continue to assume that the purpose of education is the happiness of those who get it. The improvement of society is a dreary theme unless we say that we want each member of it to be better in himself.

* From an address, "The Teacher to the Student," delivered at a symposium on the occasion of the inauguration of Richard G. Gettell as President of Mt. Holyoke College, November 9, 1957.

THE COLLEGE REPUTATION FOR
REENFORCING LEARNING

The firm establishment of an institutional reputation for being centered on a solid learning program is an enormous advantage. Here nothing succeeds like success. The reputation for advancing sound learning has its own independent momentum. To have achieved this state of academic grace means for any college that its battle for a wholesome climate is three-quarters won. It needs only to have the line held and the reputation revalidated from year to year through the achievements of its teachers and students.

In the years ahead this solid repute will be even more respected by young people. The reputation for serious work is already striking a responsive chord with many earnest young people in many institutions. And a kind of natural selection and gravitation of students who would be serious workers already operates to help achieve and maintain that climate. There are splendid examples today of fine colleges. One can surely point to Swarthmore, Oberlin, or Amherst, in the liberal arts, and the Massachusetts Institute of Technology, in engineering, as examples of places where to enter is a learning distinction and to remain is an evidence that genuine individual learning is being achieved. Under conditions such as these many a campus can arrive at a truer cultural unity and pride of status among teachers and students.

The slogan therefore should be: Build the right reputation, and good students and good education will follow.

But this repute can no longer be in terms solely of the high

I.Q. of applicants and students. Colleges will continue to have divergent objectives. But they will all subscribe to the forward aims of high zeal and distinctive creative and intellectual attainment. What is to be expected and worked for is the maximum effort of each student according to his special capabilities. The challenge today is to engender excitement for the life of the mind among the *average* students.

❦

LEARNING HOW VERSUS LEARNING WHAT

The reader may be eager to remind me that attention thus far has been centered on the *how* of learning, in an institutional as well as a personal sense, with hardly a reference to *what* is to be learned. That the *what* of learning is crucial to facilitating the *how* should by this point have become clear; for improvement in the learning climate is obviously contingent upon the relevance of what the student is being asked to learn in curricular and other terms.

I cannot, however, elaborate here on curricular objectives in higher education. Nor is it easy to proffer a summary view of my own convictions on such basic issues.* There are many ways of stating the case, all having to do with the relation of the young person's life to his own maturation, to his capacity to cope with the world of nature, to his social competence as a citizen, to his sense of reverence.

The goals of education and the means to reach them are

* A considerable array of descriptive facts is to be found in *Goals for American Education,* edited by Bryson, Finkelstein, and MacIver (New York: Harper & Brothers, 1950); see especially my own Chapter XVII, "The Role of Objectives in Higher Education."

always interdependent. Attractive and valid objectives make learning more attractive and valid. The learning effort meets less resistance and enlists enthusiasm when that which is to be learned is realized as relevant and indigenous to the individual's growth process, to his aspirations toward selfhood, and to the sense of a shared responsibility in an always enlarging society of one's peers.

I have assumed that what we educate for may be answered in many ways, but that there is a central focus on personal growth, social competence, and creativity, allied to the clear aims and learning climate of a college or university.

❦

CONCLUSION

Having confined myself preponderantly to a recital of ways and means, I want to conclude by stressing greater attention to inwardness in the search for knowledge.

The consummations of learning as they continue can help to achieve a natural transcendence in mind and spirit, a growing selfhood that is embraced by each individual for its greater rewards.

The pursuit of learning presumes commitment to a serious view of life. Earnestness of purpose and a responsible quest for learning are not, however, to be confused with being somber, joyless, or stuffy. Rather we seek to infuse a certain cheerful "toughness," in making plain that the price at which the gods sell excellence is in the sweat of the brow.

Surely our adult awareness of the confused national scene and the even more recalcitrant international complex prompts us to sobriety and offers patriotic reasons for getting down to business. We need not apologize for seriousness here; and never was any grudging attitude less in evidence in our classrooms.

One question is central as the student enrolls for study: How can adults enlist his natural zest for learning most quickly to his own advantage as a future personality and citizen?

If today's youth seems less idealistic than older people would wish, to assign blame is idle. If the tensions of the present and immediate future are channeled toward evoking patriotic and high ethical and religious interests and ideals, the response promises to be heartening. Appeals to a sense of duty and to the summons of public service can still be attractive. We have probably asked too little and expected less in a world where youthful idealism is always eager to be catalyzed if the appeal is compelling. Here, therefore, building on the foundation of college learning can be an intellectual, moral, and spiritual cause of the highest priority.

It will be important that college leadership keeps attuned to —and imaginatively ahead of—the growing seriousness on the part of students. The climate of true learning should thus come to be deeply structured so as to give heart and substance to the serious mood of the times we face.

Let us frankly capitalize through such a program upon this appeal to idealism. Let us give the lead to this quality of student-striving now ready to become manifest.

And let us do this strong in the realization that as young people accept willingly the invitation to learning, they are preparing to become co-workers in a democratic society. The inwardness of learning is self-command—command of the intellectual resources that will build toward a community of free men in a tolerable world society.

For the college should wisely propose to constitute itself to provide maximum opportunity for that autonomous individual growth which is democracy's gain and need. A program of free, untrammeled but committed learning in the appropriate areas is the apotheosis of a democratic fulfillment. And it is the heart of the college objective. Given a new and unified faculty vision of its own leadership, the college can become possessed of deeper purposiveness. And the students will rally to a learning effort that will give vibrancy and unprecedented glamour to the claims and uses of contemporary scholarship.

In short, the weather report might be that the climate of learning in higher education seems clearing and promises fair.

Let Woodrow Wilson from a Harvard Phi Beta Kappa lecture* supply with stirring appositeness a summary of my message:

My plea then is this, that we now deliberately set ourselves to make a home for the spirit of learning; that we reorganize our colleges on the lines of this simple conception, that a college is not only a body of studies but a mode of association. . . . It must become a community of scholars and pupils—a free community but a very real one, in which democracy may work its reasonable triumphs of accommodation, its vital processes of union.

* Quoted in an address by Burton P. Fowler, "The Human Side of Education," Harvard Summer Session, July 9, 1957.

Set in Linotype Fairfield
Format by Marguerite Swanton
Manufactured by The Haddon Craftsmen, Inc.
Published by HARPER & BROTHERS, New York